Now I Know

Checkup

MW01070109

by MELVIN AND GILDA BERGER

SCHOLASTIC INC.

New York   Toronto   London   Auckland   Sydney

Mexico City   New Delhi   Hong Kong   Buenos Aires

ISBN 10: 0-439-02448-X
ISBN 13: 978-0-439-02448-8

Text copyright © 2007 by Melvin and Gilda Berger.
All rights reserved. Published by Scholastic Inc.
SCHOLASTIC, NOW I KNOW readers, and associated logos
are trademarks and/or registered trademarks of Scholastic Inc.

12 11 10 9 8 7 6 5 4 3 2 1   7 8 9 10 11 12/0

Printed in the U.S.A.
First Printing, September 2007
Book design by Nancy Sabato

Hello, doctor.

You get a checkup every year.

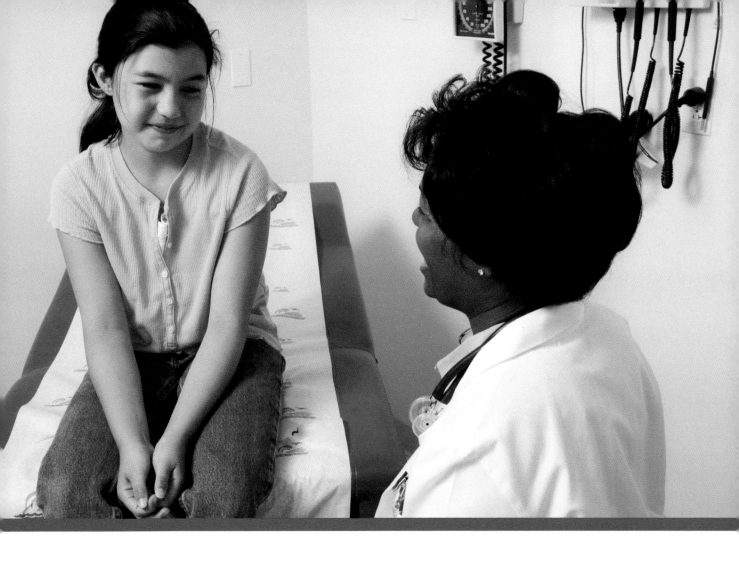

Hop up on the table.

Let's check your weight.

Let's check
your height.

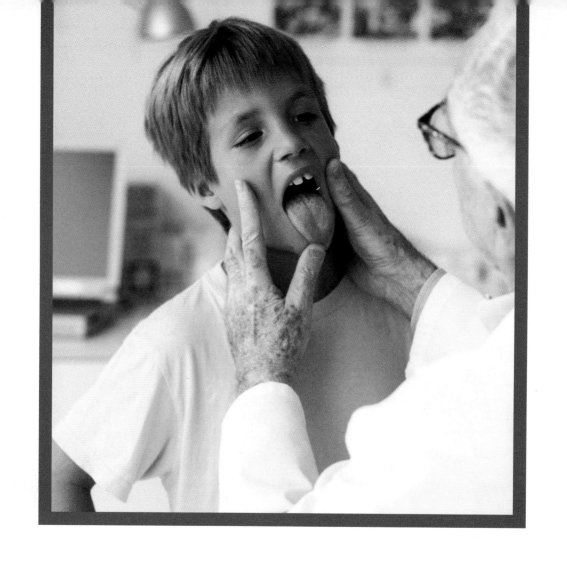

Stick out your tongue.

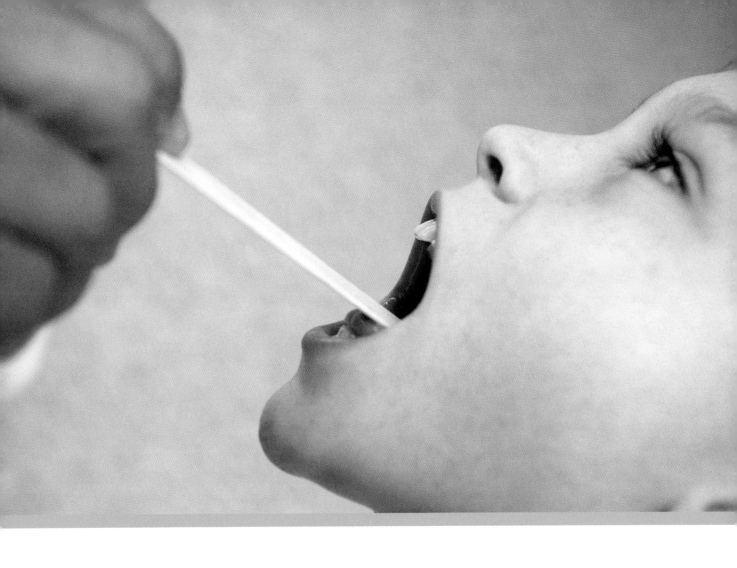

Say Ahhhh.

The doctor feels your neck

and looks in your ears.

ZOOM!

ZOOM!

The doctor checks your eyes.

You will read the eye chart.

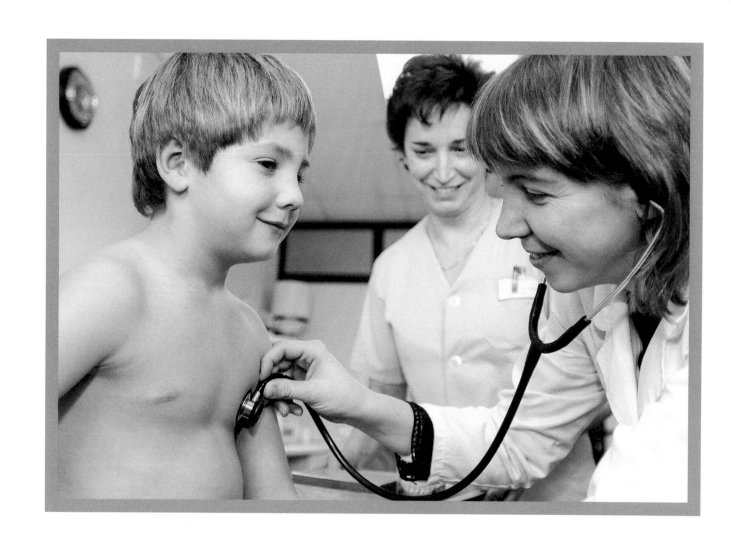

How's your heart?

The doctor checks your blood pressure.

DID YOU KNOW?

Your foot kicks when the doctor taps your knee.

Tap on the knee.

The doctor presses your belly.

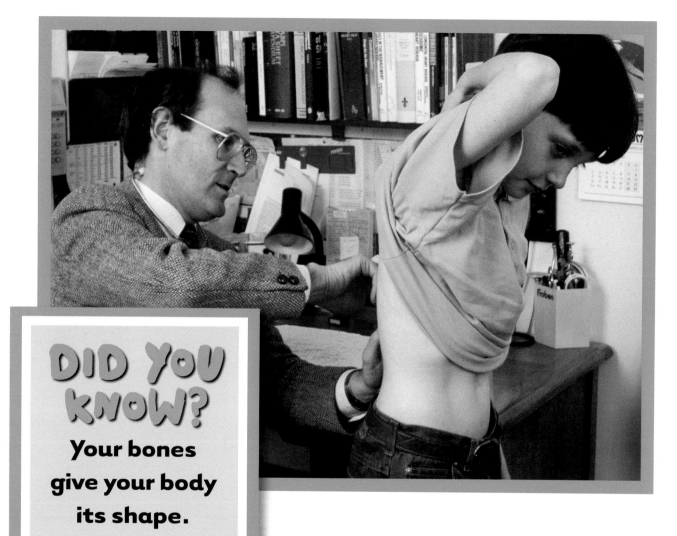

DID YOU KNOW?

Your bones give your body its shape.

Let's check your bones.

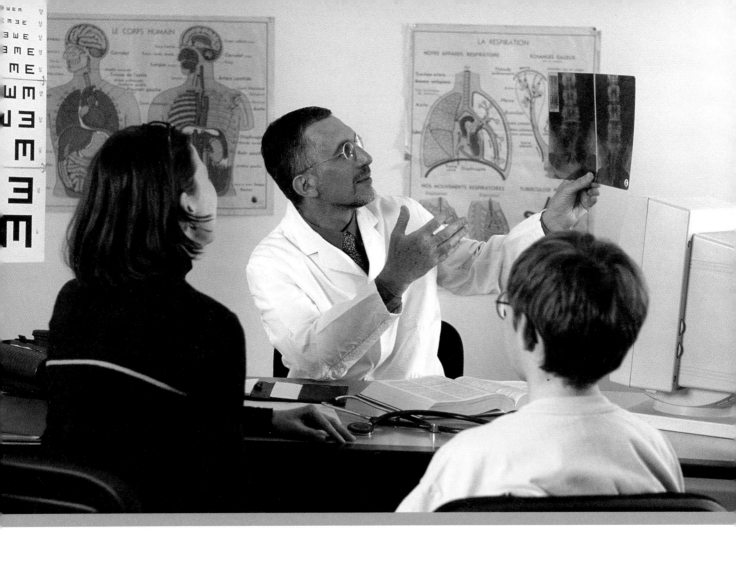

You may need an X-ray.

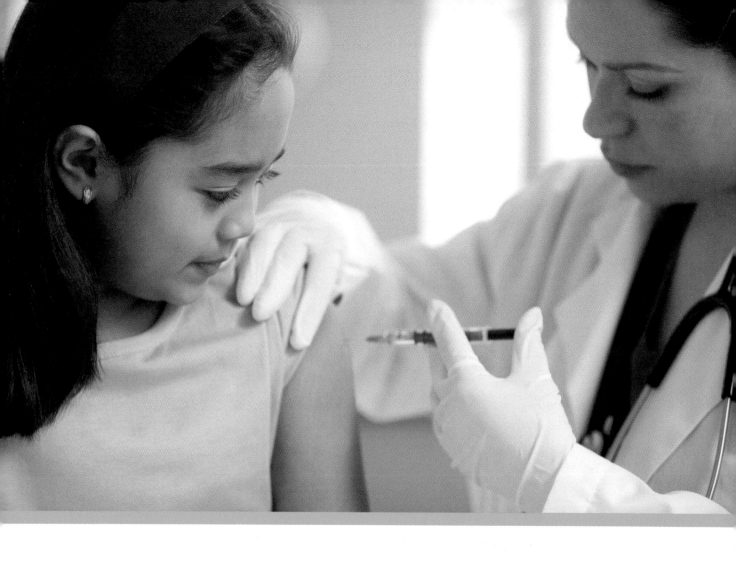

A shot helps keep you healthy.

Everything is fine.
See you next year.

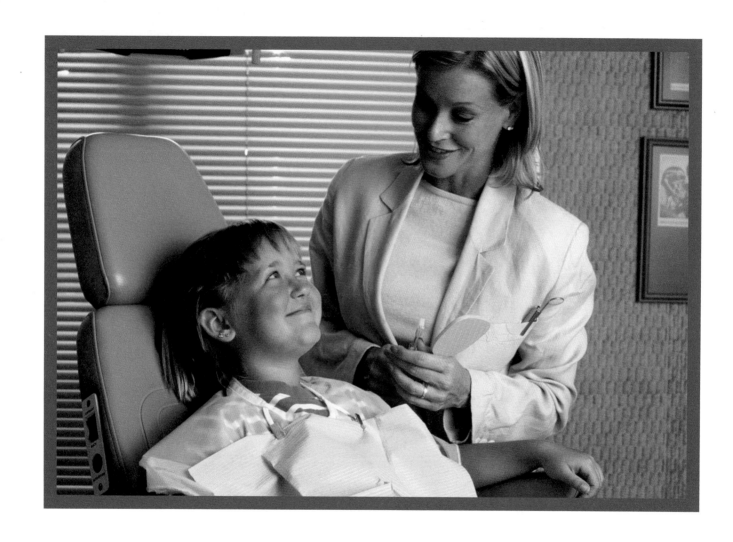

Now a checkup with the dentist.

The dentist gets ready.

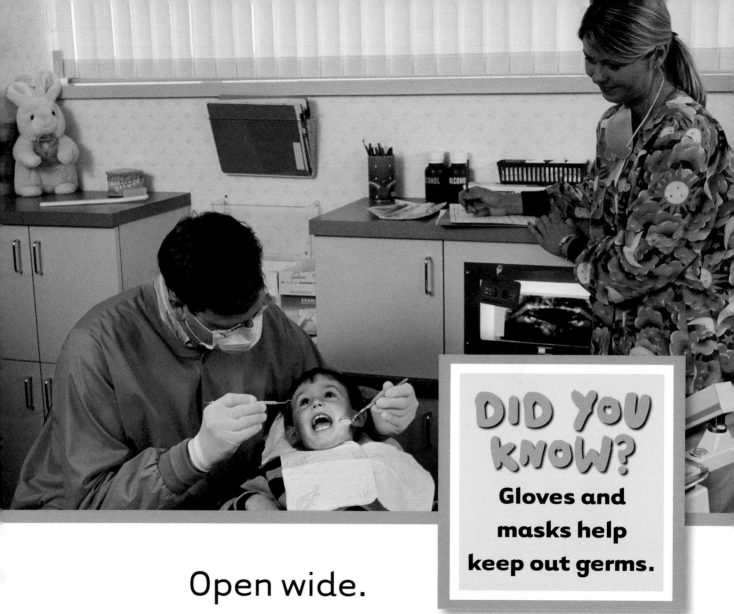

DID YOU KNOW?

Gloves and masks help keep out germs.

Open wide.

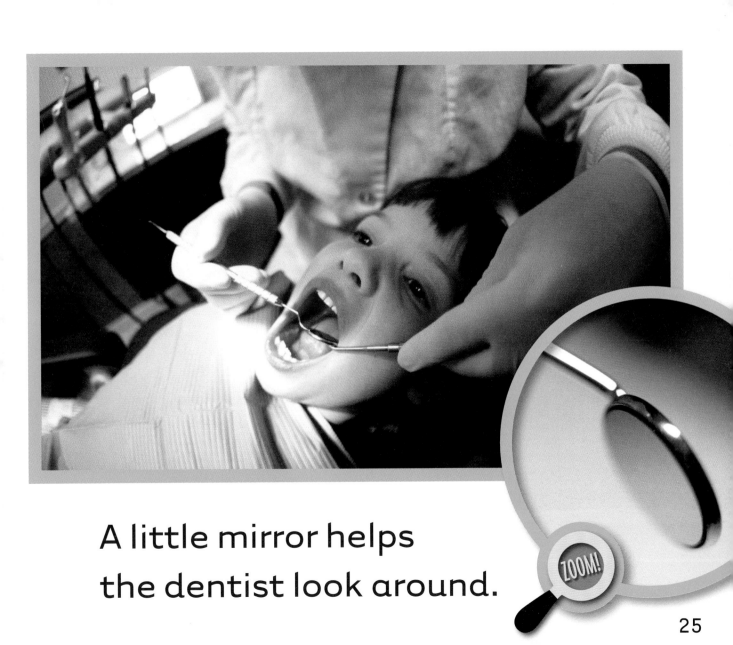

A little mirror helps
the dentist look around.

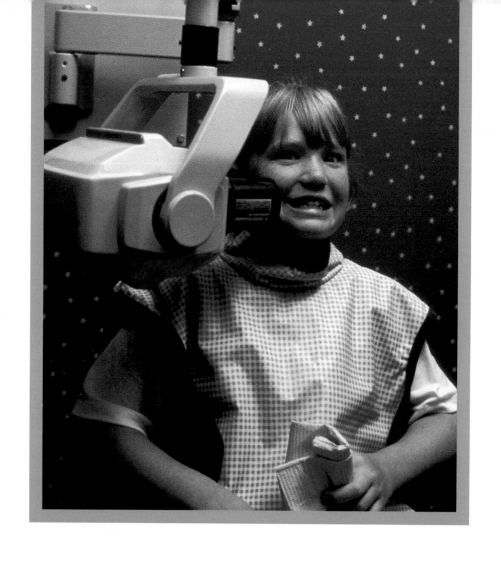

The dentist may X-ray your teeth.

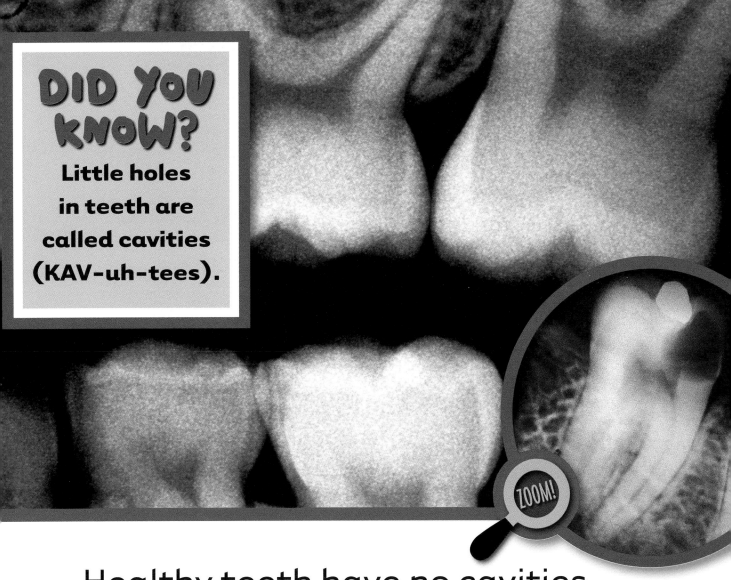

ZOOM!

Healthy teeth have no cavities.

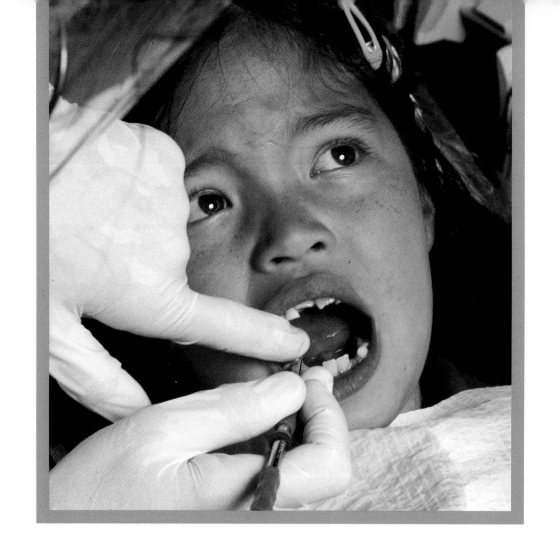

The dentist cleans your teeth.

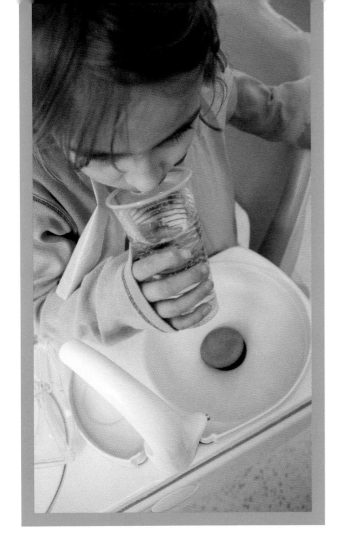

Swish, swish, swish. Then spit.

Brush carefully.

Stay healthy!

GLOSSARY

Blood pressure: The force of blood as it flows through your body.

Cavities: Holes or hollow spaces in teeth.

Dentist: A doctor who takes care of your teeth.

Doctor: A person trained to keep you healthy and treat you when you are sick.

Germs: Tiny living beings that can make you sick.

Heart: The organ that pumps blood through your body.

Height: A measure of how tall you are.

Muscles: The parts of your body that help you move.

Physician: Another word for doctor.

Weight: A measure of how heavy you are.

X-ray: A picture of the inside of a person's body.